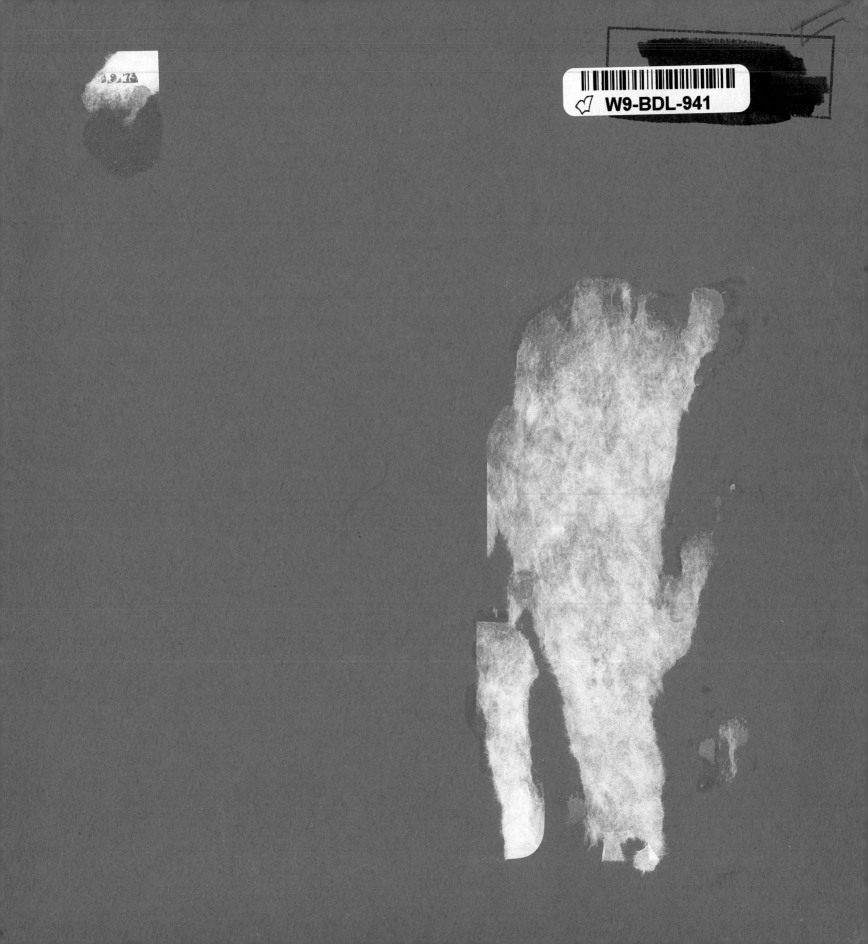

*ivory dipper*, Museum of the American Indian, photograph by Carmelo Guadagno

*Shaman's doll*, Museum of the American Indian, photograph by Alfred H. Tamarin

HARPER & ROW, PUBLISHERS

NEW YORK, EVANSTON, AND LONDON

# THE
# ART
## OF THE
# ESKIMO

## SHIRLEY GLUBOK

DESIGNED BY
**OSCAR KRAUSS**

SPECIAL PHOTOGRAPHY BY
**ALFRED H. TAMARIN**

THE AUTHOR GRATEFULLY ACKNOWLEDGES THE ASSISTANCE OF:

FREDERICK DOCKSTADER, Director, Museum of the American Indian, Heye Foundation

LOUISE CONDIT, Assistant Dean in Charge of the Junior Museum, The Metropolitan Museum of Art

S. H. RIESENBERG, Curator, Division of Ethnology, U.S. National Museum, Smithsonian Institution

BARBARA GARRISON of the Spence School, New York

Master PETER SELWYN

●

*Other Books By SHIRLEY GLUBOK:*

THE ART OF ANCIENT EGYPT
THE ART OF LANDS IN THE BIBLE
THE ART OF ANCIENT GREECE
THE ART OF THE NORTH AMERICAN INDIAN

●

Not far from the North Pole, on the frozen shores of the Arctic Ocean, live a hardy, cheerful people we call Eskimos. They call themselves *Innuit,* which means *the people.* Eskimo is an Indian word meaning *the eaters of raw flesh.*

The Eskimos live in parts of Siberia, Alaska, Canada, and Greenland. Life is very hard in these cold, icy lands. The winters are long and dark, and for several months of the year the sun never shines.

Every Eskimo man is a hunter. Animals provide him with everything he needs: food, clothing, and shelter. Almost all Eskimo art shows the hunter or the animals he hunts.

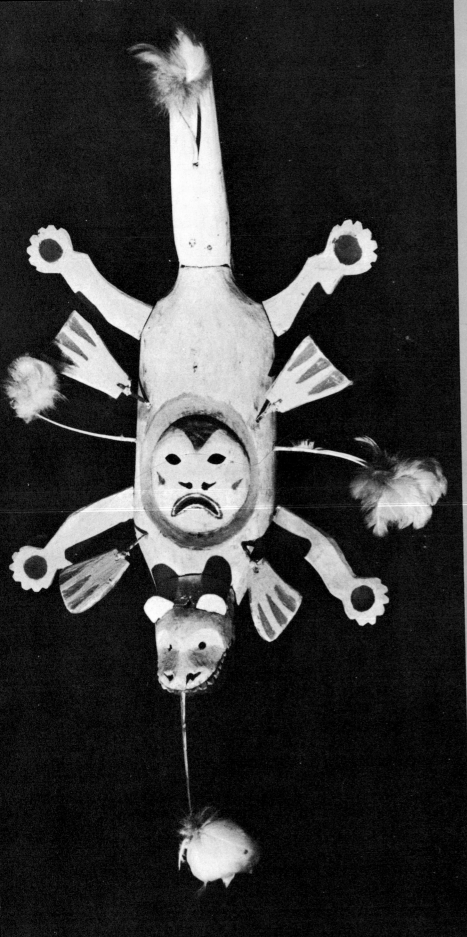

Museum of the American Indian, photograph by Alfred H. Tamarin

Trees cannot grow in the frozen northern lands, so Eskimos have very little wood. They carefully collect driftwood washed in by the rivers and the sea. The Alaskan Eskimos use the driftwood to make masks, which are worn for dancing ceremonies.

The Eskimos believe that every animal has a spirit. On the left is a bear mask. The bear's spirit looks out from the circle on its back. On the right is a walrus mask. The spirit of the walrus is shown between tusks on the forehead.

These masks are painted, and they are decorated with feathers and fur.

State Museum, West Berli

6

Rasmussen Collection, Portland Art Museum

Museum of the American Indian, photograph by Carmelo Guadagno

The Eskimo hunter wears masks in magic dances to honor the animals he has caught. He does not want their spirits to be angry. He wishes to please them so that many more animals will come during the next hunting season.

The mask on the left is in the shape of a bird. Its spirit is carved on the breast. Hands, legs, feathers, fish, and other objects hang from rings around the spirit.

The curious animal mask above is carved simply in an ancient style of Eskimo art.

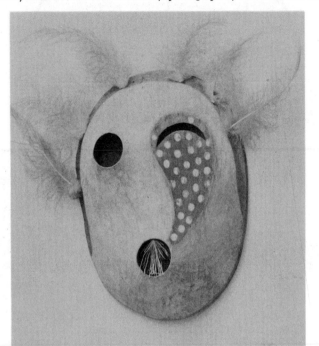

The Eskimos also believe in evil spirits which live in lonely and far-off places. The spirits are thought to bring sickness and bad luck. Medicine men, called *shamans,* wear special masks to keep these evil spirits from doing harm.

The shaman mask on the left is both jolly and fearsome. Eskimo art is often happy and sad at the same time.

There are many masks like the one above showing one of the evil spirits.

The spirit mask on the left looks bright and cheerful with its laughing mouth and big round eyes.

Sometimes Eskimos use masks just for fun. They hold contests between villages, trying to make one another laugh. They wear comedy masks like the one below and clown about with funny motions. The audience tries to keep from laughing. Later the villages exchange gifts.

These Eskimo masks can be worn over a person's face, but some are so big that they are hung from the ceiling. Someone stands behind the large ones to make them move.

Ivory carving is the oldest Eskimo art. Most Eskimo ivory comes from the long, curved tusks of the walrus.

First the carver holds the ivory tusk in his hand and turns it this way and that. He talks to it. He hums a song. The Eskimo believes that there is a shape already in the ivory, and he wants to find out what it is. He cuts away the parts of the ivory that hide the shape waiting inside the tusk.

An Eskimo carver found the shape of this bird waiting inside a piece of ivory.

The circle of figures on the right was cut from the round hollow root of a walrus tusk. Very little care was taken in shaping the bodies, but the figures are lively and joyful. Eskimo artists usually take less care in carving people than animals.

Royal Ontario Museum, University of Toro

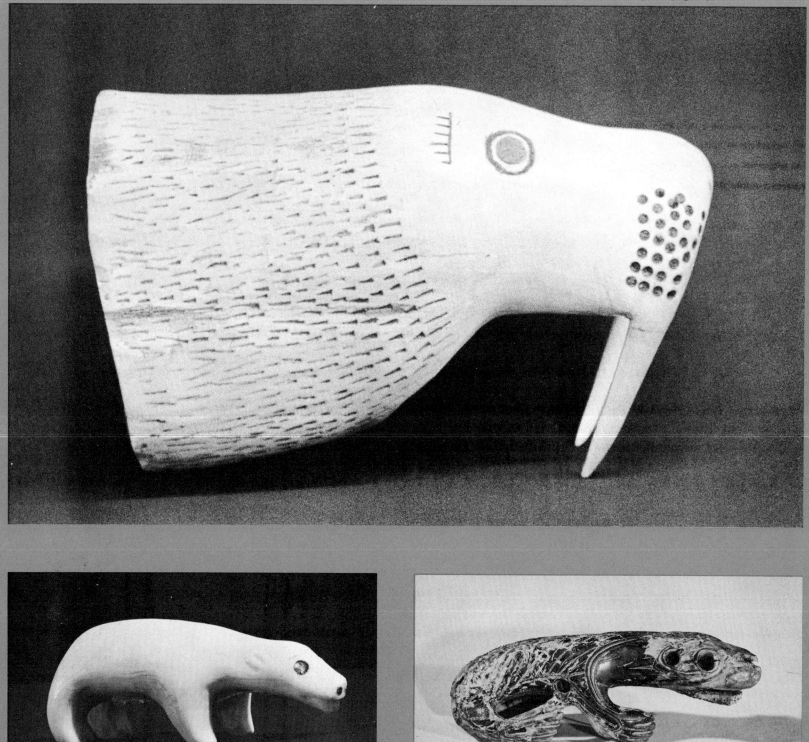

Smithsonian Institution, photograph by Alfred H. Tamarin

Carlebach Gallery, Inc., photograph by Alfred H. Tamarin

American Museum of Natural History

Eskimo men are expert hunters. During the long, dark winters when they cannot go out, they carve little ivory figures of animals. They think that the carvings will bring them luck in the hunt.

This walrus head is simply and strongly shaped. The eyes, whiskers, and fur have been cut into the ivory. The baby polar bear has no little lines, or details, cut into it. The carving is smooth and graceful.

Old ivory, found under the frozen ground, is called *fossil ivory*. Some fossil ivory comes from the tusks of mammoths, huge animals that lived thousands of years ago. The baby walrus is more than a thousand years old. The ivory is discolored from being buried a long time.

Eskimos keep their ivory carvings wrapped in animal skins. The little ivory statues are unwrapped and passed around when guests come or when children gather for a story. The figures are supposed to be handled and looked at from every side.

Above is an ivory carving of a seal, the most important animal to the Eskimo. Seals provide him with meat for food, oil for heat and light, and skins for clothing.

The Eskimo travels over ice and snow on his sled. Below is an ivory carving of a sled pulled by a reindeer. The antlers were attached separately, but they have been lost. A reindeer pulling a sled recalls the story of Santa Claus, or St. Nicholas, traveling from the North Pole.

Pictures are often incised, or scratched, on ivory. The incised scene of a whale hunt can be seen on the ivory whale to the right.

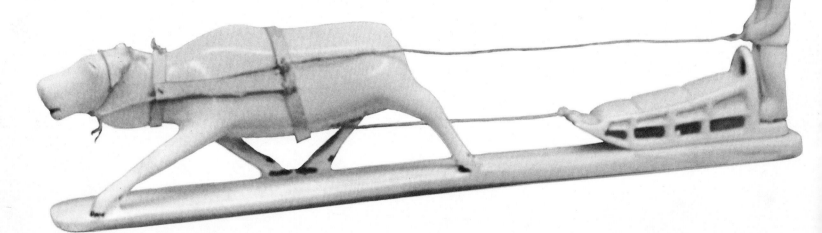

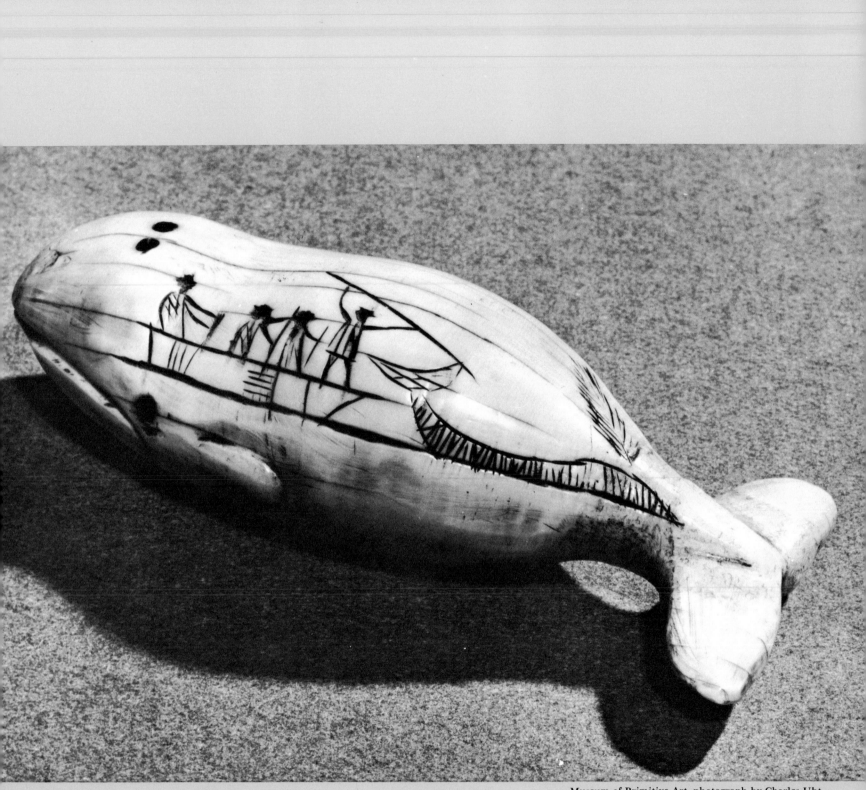

Museum of Primitive Art, photograph by Charles Uht

17

Courtesy of the Smithsonian Institution

Today Eskimo artists make carvings from a dark stone called soapstone. The stone carver has the same idea as the ivory carver. He believes that the shape he will carve is already in the stone. He holds the stone in his hand, waiting for it to whisper to him. What shape will be set free? He uses metal tools to bring out the figures.

The soapstone hunter on the left is dragging home a seal. The hunter on the right caught a seal and a fish. The fish is carved out of ivory.

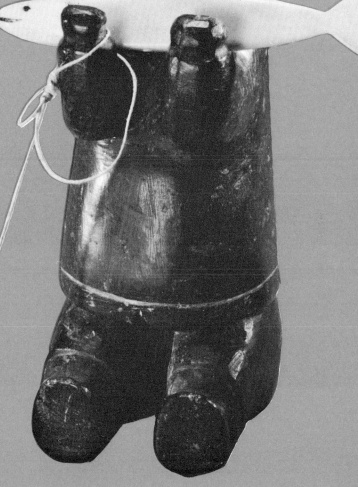

American Museum of Natural History

19

*Walrus,* National Museum of Canada

*Snowy owl and chicks,* National Museum of Canada

The carver usually finishes his work on the same day that he starts it. When he finishes, he smooths the stone carving with another stone. Then he soaks it in seal oil for a few days. Afterward he rubs it with his hands to make it shine. Most stone carvings are made by Canadian Eskimos.

On the right is a finger mask, worn by Eskimo women for special dances. It is carved of wood and decorated with fur and feathers. Finger masks fit on the first two fingers. The women stand still and move only their hands and arms. The little masks seem to dance and talk and laugh like puppets.

*Narwhal,* National Museum of Canada

Museum of the American Indian, photograph by Alfred H. Tamar

Peabody Museum, Harvard University, photograph by Alfred H. Tamarin

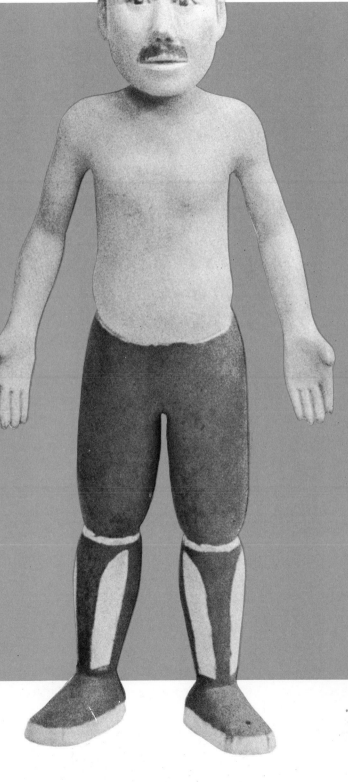

Alaskan Eskimos dance in public huts called dance houses. Most dances are held to honor the spirits of the animals of the hunt. Sometimes they are held to entertain visitors from other villages during the terribly cold and stormy winters.

The four wooden dancing figures on the left are alive with action. Their whole bodies are in motion, and they seem to leap and jump to the dance rhythm. The seated figures are singing and beating drums.

The figure on the right is a wooden model of an Eskimo dancer.

Smithsonian Institution, photograph by Alfred H. Tamarin

On the left is a doll mask, hung with gay figures of people and birds.

Eskimo children like to play with ivory or wooden dolls. Little girls learn to sew dolls' clothes using the skins of reindeer and seals.

Eskimo mothers carry their babies inside their furred hoods. The mother doll is wearing clothing of reindeer skin, which is warm but not heavy. The shirt and hood are called a parka. The parka is worn with the fur on the inside. The long shirttail makes the parka extra warm. The trousers are worn fur-side out.

The man doll is dressed in water-proof clothes made from seal gut. The circle-and-dot decoration makes this a handsome parka.

American Museum of Natural History

Museum of the American Indian, photograph by Carmelo Guadagno

The Eskimos have gotten many ideas from whalers, explorers, and fur traders. One thing these adventurers taught the Eskimos is that walrus tusks could be carved into pipes. The pipes are made to be sold or traded. Pictures of Eskimo life are incised on the sides of the pipes. Soot, clay, or animal blood is rubbed into the lines to make the pictures stand out.

The pipe above is incised with pictures of hunters, reindeer, polar bears, seals, and whales. The top of it is carved with figures of a dog sled, seals, and walruses.

The pipe below is beautifully decorated with lively figures of men, animals, and birds. The tobacco goes into the bowl of the pipe, which is made of bone.

Many Eskimo pipes were never meant to be smoked. They are works of art, made to be looked at.

Each of these pipes was made from a single piece of ivory. They were cut out of the thickest part of walrus tusks.

The elaborate pipe at the top shows a whaling ship with its sails spread. There are also a rowboat, a reindeer, walruses, birds, and other objects on the top and sides.

The pipe in the middle has the simple circle-and-dot design that has been used in Eskimo art since ancient times. This design is both beautiful and easy to make.

The third pipe has carvings of human figures and animals. The men and boys are pulling a line. Ducks, birds, and seals are carved on the top and along the sides.

Museum of the American Indian, photograph by Alfred H. Tamarin

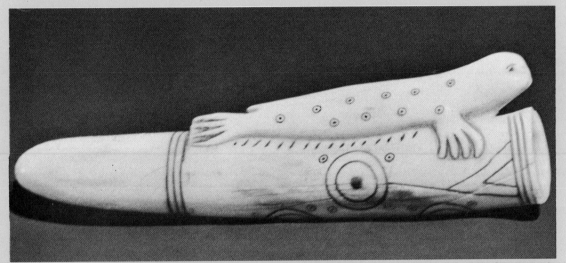

Carlebach Gallery, Inc., photograph by Alfred H. Tamarin

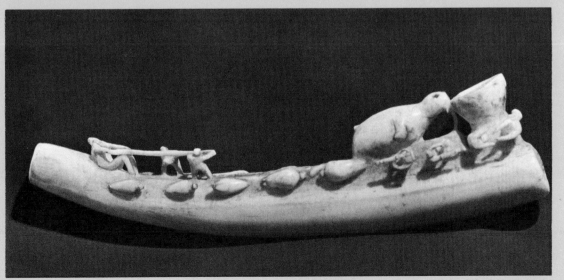

Carlebach Gallery, Inc., photograph by Alfred H. Tamarin

29

Everything is scarce in the lands of the Eskimos. Therefore nothing can be wasted. Every scrap of material—even animal bone—is put to use.

The man on the left is carved out of spongy whalebone. He is wearing a fur hat and his eyes are ivory. His mustache and eyebrows are painted.

The miniature dog sled is made of a harder kind of bone. The Eskimos invented the dog sled for travel over ice and snow.

These graceful geese are carved of whalebone.

Eskimos use ivory rods to keep records of important events. These rods, called record sticks, tell a story in pictures.

This record stick tells of hunters and how they traveled and found their animals. The figures are lively in this busy scene. The animals look surprised

by the coming of the hunters. These tiny incised drawings are fine miniature art. The record stick should be turned around and studied from every side. Figures are drawn upside down or right side up.

The ivory carving on the right is a calendar. It is in the form of a man who looks like a trader. The round buttons in the center of his coat may stand for six days of the week. The design above them probably stands for Sunday. The figure is double, and each side shows six months of the year.

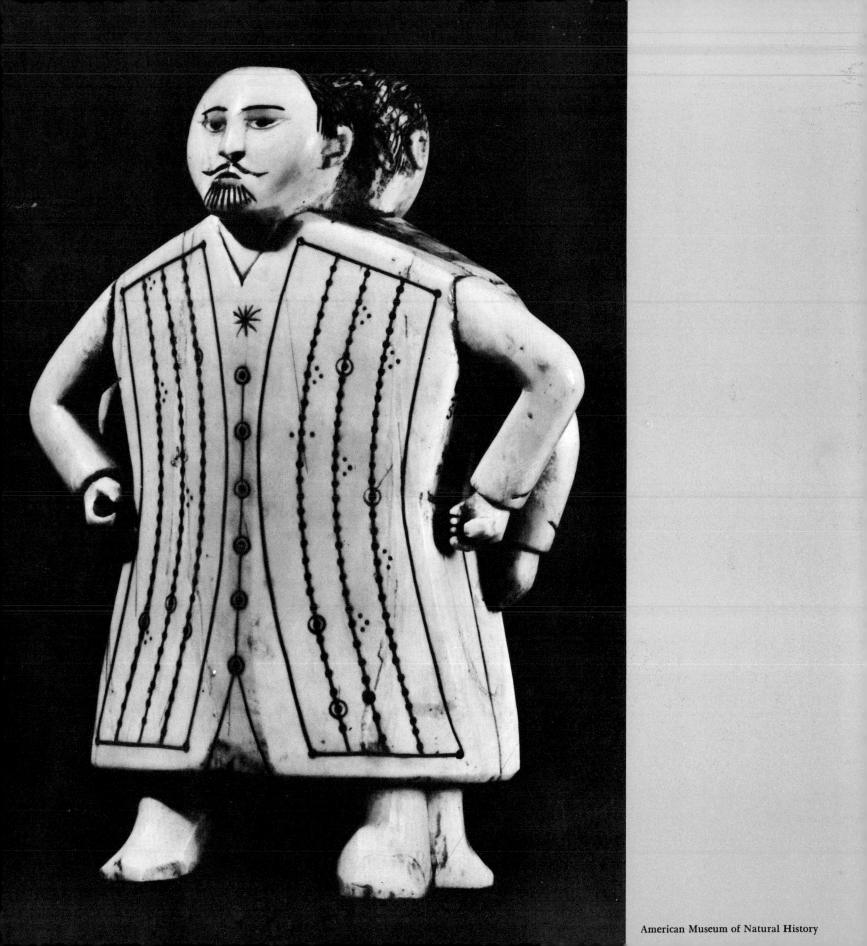

Godthåb Museum, Greenland, Courtesy Danish Information Office

The first Eskimos to use paper for their art were the Greenlanders. Over a hundred years ago a Greenland Eskimo named Aron from Kangek made this woodcut for a book of legends. The legends had been handed down from father to son for generations.

The picture shows a hunter who has tamed a bear and taught it to pull his sled. He is getting ready to feed it seal meat. The bear looks hungry, waiting to be fed. The drawing has simple, strong lines, like the ivory carvings. The hunter is shown in movement; the other figures are still.

The picture shows one kind of Eskimo house, dug partly into the earth. The clothes and the way many Eskimos wear their hair can also be seen.

Musée du Québec, photograph by Alfred H. Tamarin

Today Canadian Eskimos use paper to make prints. The picture of an archer pointing his arrow at flying birds is a sealskin stencil print. The design was cut out in sealskin to make the stencil. The stencil was placed on paper. Then the color was brushed through the cutout designs onto the paper. Stiff polar bear hair makes excellent stencil brushes.

The picture above is a stone print. The design was carved into a flat block of stone. Then ink was brushed onto the design, and paper was placed onto the stone and gently rubbed.

Sometimes useful objects are carved out of ivory. On the left is a snuff box, made by hollowing out a section of a walrus tusk. The box is beautifully decorated with incised drawings. The thin handle is made of animal skin.

On the right, above, is a scraper decorated with a lively scene of a whale hunt. The handle of the scraper is modern, but the blade is very old. It is made of jade, a hard stone. The scraper was used to clean the skins of animals caught by the hunter. The skins had to be scraped and dried before they were sewn together for clothing.

The cribbage board, below, was made by Eskimo carvers to sell to traders from other lands. It is used to keep the score in a card game called cribbage.

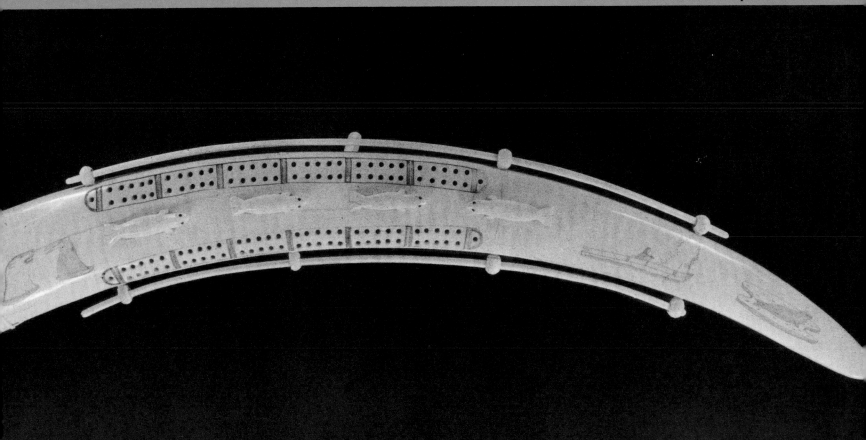

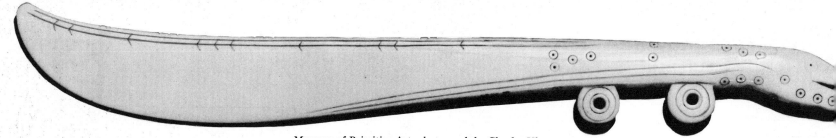

Museum of Primitive Art, photograph by Charles Uht

Eskimo men use ivory snow knives to build houses called *igloos*. The knife above is a toy that was used by Eskimo children to make animals and birds of snow. The children have make-believe hunts, using toy snow knives.

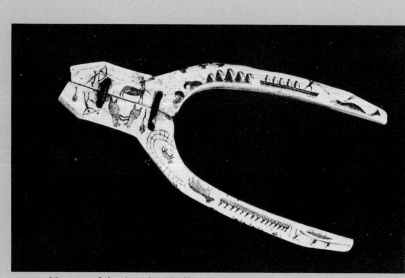

Museum of the American Indian, photograph by Alfred H. Tamarin

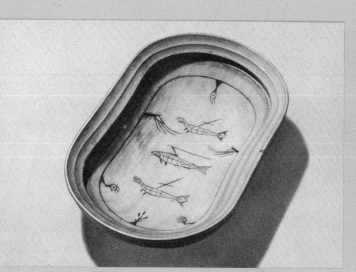

Museum of Primitive Art, photograph by Charles Uht

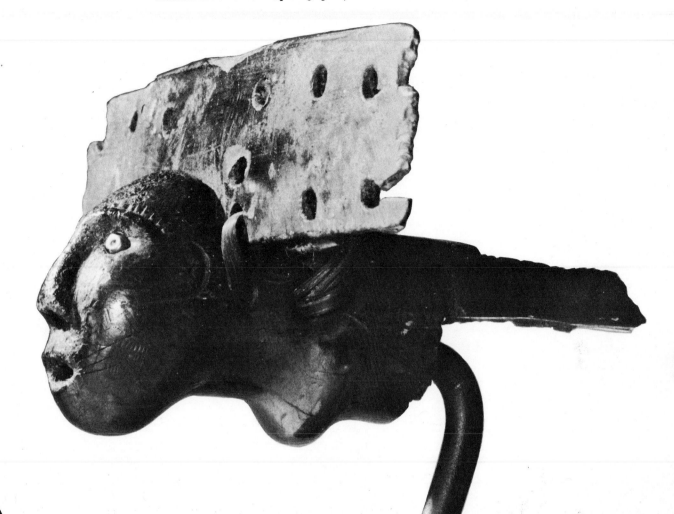

Oarlocks are used in *umiaks*—family boats rowed by the women—to hold the oars in place. On the far left is an ivory oarlock that is completely covered with drawings of the hunt.

The wooden bowl on the left is decorated in the same style used in carving ivory.

This powerful carving of a face is the handle of an Eskimo drum. It is made of fossil ivory. Beads were used for eyes in order to make the face seem alive. Part of the rim of the drum is still attached.

Museum of the American Indian, photograph by Carmelo Guadagno

Eskimo hunters from southwest Alaska were proud to own wooden hats like this one. It was worn on the open seas to keep the glare of the sun out of the hunter's eyes. The hat was made from a thin board. First the board was steamed; then it was bent into the shape of a cone.

Ivory carvings of seals and whales are fastened to the hat. The carvings are thought to be magic. They are supposed to bring luck in the hunt.

This is a model of a hunting and fishing boat from the Aleutian Islands. It is called a *bidarka*. It is like a *kayak*, the one-man boat, but it has extra seats. Kayaks and bidarkas are made of skins, stretched over a narrow wooden frame. The hunter wears waterproof sealskin clothes. He sits in a hole and ties waterproof skins around his waist. The boats can skim over the open sea in heavy spray and rain. No water can get in, even if they turn over.

These four carvings are all of wood. The seal's head on the left is very lifelike. It is a decoy helmet, worn by a hunter to sneak up on a seal resting in the sun. The hunter hoped that the seal would think this was just another seal. Then the animal would not be frightened away.

Eskimo stories have been handed down from father to son for hundreds of years. They are filled with imaginary creatures that have magic power over the winds, seas, and animals. On the left is a creature from Eskimo mythology. It is part human, part seal, and part four-legged animal.

44

The wolf mask has snow goggles painted around its eyes. Snow goggles were invented by the Eskimos to protect their eyes from the bright glare of the sun on the snow and ice.

Below the wolf is a model of a hunter and his dog in a kayak. The hunter's head and arms are movable. Bright-blue beads were set in for eyes. This may have been a toy for an Eskimo boy.

The dog in the kayak is made of ivory. Dogs are very important to Eskimos. They would not be able to hunt in the winter if dogs did not pull their sleds. Eskimo dogs are a special hardy breed.

Collection of the Newark Museum    photograph by Alfred H. Tamarin

Museum of the American Indian, photograph by Alfred H. Tamarin

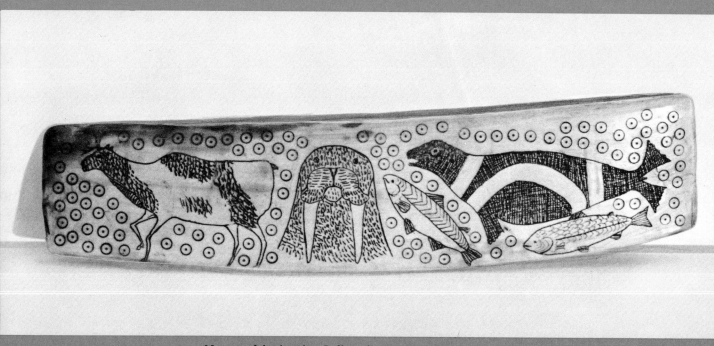

Museum of the American Indian, photograph by Alfred H. Tamarin

This is an ivory scraper, used to clean animal hides. It is decorated with very fine incised drawings. The seal, the fish, and the reindeer are clear and strong. Animals are usually shown in side view, but the walrus, in the center, is full face. The ancient Eskimo design of dots and circles makes the figures seem to be swimming.

Shamans have special dolls for their magic dances and ceremonies. The incised drawings above are from an ivory shaman's doll. The fish and birds are imaginary creatures. Some of them are upside down because the doll was meant to be looked at from all sides. The strong lines of the carvings can be clearly seen.

The years are hard for the Eskimos. They live in the most difficult part of the world with endless snow and ice. Yet art plays an important part in the lives of the people.

They have few materials but use them with great skill. They consider their art magical. People everywhere find it beautiful. The art of the Eskimo reflects the lives and interests of these strong and cheerful people.

Rasmussen Collection, Portland Art Museum

*ory dipper*, Museum of the American Indian, photograph by Carmelo Guadagno